HISTORIC HOUSTON HOW TO SEE IT

100 YEARS & 100 MILES of DAY TRIPS

LUCINDA FREEMAN

iUniverse, Inc.
Bloomington

D0366178

iUniverse books may be ordered through booksellers or by contacting:

iUniverse
1663 Liberty Drive
Bloomington, IN 47403
www.iuniverse.com
1-800-Authors (1-800-288-4677)

ISBN: 978-1-4502-7509-5 (sc)
ISBN: 978-1-4502-7511-8 (hc)
ISBN: 978-1-4502-7510-1 (ebook)

Library of Congress Control Number: 2011901925

Printed in the United States of America

iUniverse rev. date: 4/25/2011

To my parents, for their love of history and their passion for lifelong learning.

Preface

What Houston lacks in years, it makes up in dramatic events and colorful personalities. An attitude of risk taking and independence had taken hold many decades before the famous oil boom of the early 1900s made Big Oil synonymous with Texas. As early as the 1820s, settlers from Midwestern and Eastern states—and some from as far away as Canada and Europe—colonized a wide swath of Mexican territory, including what became Houston and Texas. After much friction with Mexico, Texas earned her independence at the Battle of San Jacinto in 1836, the same year the city of Houston was founded. Texas became the twenty-eighth state in 1846 and seceded with the Confederacy in 1861. Texas rejoined the Union in 1870.

It is worth noting how closely in time these events took place. Take the life of Sam Houston, the first president of the Republic of Texas, who experienced Texas under four flags: Mexico, the Republic of Texas, the United States, and the Confederacy. Before coming to Texas, Houston fought in the War of 1812. As an army general, he led Texas to her independence as a republic in 1836. Later he became governor of the newly annexed state of Texas. In 1861 he was thrown out of office for opposing secession. Had he lived until the end of the Civil War, he would have seen a fifth transition, the return of Texas to the Union.

It is my intent to bring the Houston region's history to life by highlighting influential personalities and key historical events, accompanied by day-trip itineraries for tying them together. Along the way I will corroborate some stereotypes and challenge others. I sincerely hope that you will find the book practical, educational, and entertaining ... and have half as much fun using it as I did writing it!

Contents

at New Kentucky Park. In reality, as the roads are laid out today, you need to continue east for almost six miles on 2920, turning right at Telge Road (well marked; there is a light at the intersection). Go almost nine miles. Just past the light at Cricket Hollow, turn left on **Pleasant Grove St. to enter Telge Park**. There's a marker in the parking lot.

Sam Houston's army consumed most of Matthew Burnett's chickens and grain, and they burned the fence rails. Apparently, sometime after the victory at San Jacinto, the Burnett family returned home and recovered from the whole episode. In the late 1830s and 1840s, their home became a prominent landmark and well-known tavern on the road to the city of Houston.

As you continue on Telge Road, you will shortly intersect Highway 290 and be on the northwestern outskirts of modern Houston. Heading east will take you to the center of the city. This is the end of today's guided itinerary.

Postscript: After leaving Matthew Burnett's place, Sam Houston's troops moved on to Harrisburg. On April 19 **"Deaf" Smith captured three Mexicans**, including a captain, who revealed the latest location, size, and plans of Santa Anna's army. There is a marker commemorating this capture on the Bellaire Boulevard esplanade in southwest Houston just outside Loop 610.

That key information helped Sam Houston choose his battle site and refine his strategy. The Battle of San Jacinto was only two days away.

Itinerary 3: Washington-on-the-Brazos: The Birthplace of Texas 🚲

-Including Independence and Anderson, plus Retreat Hill Winery

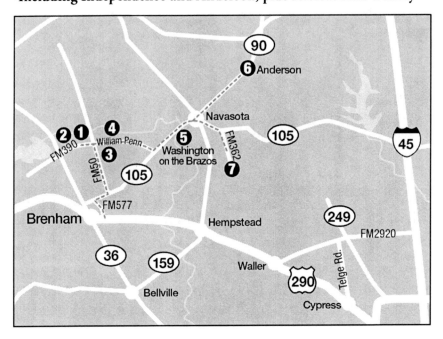

1. **Independence Baptist Church**
2. **Baylor Park**
3. **Margaret Houston homesite**
4. **Seward Plantation**
5. **Museum complex at Washington-on-the-Brazos**
6. **Anderson, Texas**
7. **Groce's Retreat/Retreat Hill Winery**

Before you go ... Note that while the **museum at Washington-on-the-Brazos** is currently open every day of the year, from 8:00 a.m. until dusk, the **Fanthorp Inn** at Anderson is officially open for guided tours only on Wednesdays through Sundays between 9:00 a.m. and 12:00 p.m. and between 1:00 and 4:00 p.m. (If you're there on Monday or Tuesday, you might get lucky and find a park ranger available for a tour; just don't count on it). The guided tour of the Fanthorp Inn is well worth the effort. The enthusiastic park rangers provide a wealth of information, and much of the structure and its furnishings are original. At this writing, the award-winning **Retreat Hill Winery** is open for tours and tastings on Bluebonnet Wine Trail weekends. Visit http://www.texasbluebonnetwinetrail.com/.

For more information on the Washington-on-the-Brazos Park, visit the Parks Department website at www.tpwd.state.tx.us or call 936-878-2214.

For more information on Fanthorp, including Stagecoach Days and other special occasions during the year, call 936-873-2633.

For more information on Retreat Hill Winery, visit www.retreathill.com or call 936-825-8282.

For information on bicycle tours in the Washington and Independence area, visit www.independencetx.com.

For food: The popular **Brenham Airport Diner**, the Southern Flyer, is open from 11:00 a.m. to 3:00 p.m. Sundays through Thursdays and 11:00 a.m. to 9:00 p.m. on Fridays and Saturdays. You'll be near it early in the itinerary, about one and a half hours from Houston. Between Washington and Anderson, near Navasota, a good eating place is **Café M. Bloomers**, on the feeder of Highway 6 just north of 105. It's open Tuesdays to Sundays from 11:00 a.m. to 4:00 p.m. In Washington, locals recommend **R Café**, near the entrance to the park, on FM 1155.

The itinerary: Start by heading northwest from Houston on Highway 290. At Brenham, turn right on FM 577/Gun and Rod Road, toward Highway 105. After three miles on 577, turn right on 105. Within two miles, turn left onto FM 50.

Most of the sites in Independence are very close to the intersection of Highways 50 and 390.

Independence's roots go back to 1824, when it was founded as **Coles Settlement. Baylor University** began here in 1845. Sam Houston's family lived here from 1853 to 1867. Margaret Houston is buried here, rather than with her husband in Huntsville, because she died of yellow fever and it was considered dangerous to move the body. This area was also a Confederate quartermaster subdepot. You'll see a marker where Hood's Brigade was organized just east of the main intersection of the highways.

In recent times, Independence has gained a reputation among coffee drinkers for being home to **Independence Coffee**, which can be found at all Whole Foods stores and some HEB stores. Their coffees, carefully roasted in small batches, include such blends as "Old 300" and Brazos Ferry. You can find out more at www.independencecoffee.com.

On your left at the northwest corner of the intersection of 50 and 390, you'll notice the old **Independence Baptist Church,** *(STOP)* **Stop 1.** It was organized in 1839, and it is the oldest active Baptist congregation in the state. Sam and Margaret Houston worshiped here. Sam was baptized in nearby Rocky Creek in 1854. When told his sins were being washed away, he expressed extreme pity for the fish downstream!

The present building was built in 1872. The church bell was donated by Nancy Lea, Sam's mother-in-law, to commemorate his conversion. The bell, cast in copper and tin, was made by Meneely Foundry in New York. Across the street, you'll see the small **Houston-Lea Family Cemetery,** where Margaret Lea Houston and her mother, Nancy Moffette Lea, are interred. Margaret died in the terrible yellow fever epidemic of 1867, which affected a wide swath of southeast Texas.

Head west on Highway 390 (it will be a right turn if you've parked at the church and you're turning around on Highway 50). In less than half a mile on your left you'll see a house and white picket fence set back from the road. This is the **site of the Houstons' home** for several years in the 1850s. The original house was built in 1837; the current house was built in 1897. The marker is inside the fence and is not visible from the highway.

Continuing west on 390, very soon you'll see the **Baylor Park** complex on your right, *(STOP)* **Stop 2,** with several historic houses in front. You can park near the structures. You'll see a marker for **John Prince Coles,** the founder of Independence, who came to Texas from North Carolina in 1821. He's one of the "Old 300." After serving in the Republic of Texas Army in 1836, he held a number of public offices, including a senate seat in the first congress of the republic.

Continuing for a short distance toward the columns of the old university, you will note that **Baylor University** was chartered by the Republic of

Texas in 1845. It is the oldest university in Texas operating under its original name. Baylor was located at this site for forty years.

According to the *Handbook of Texas Online*, Robert Emmett Bledsoe—**R. E. B. Baylor**—was a prominent leader in diverse arenas of public service: military, judicial, political, educational, fraternal, and religious. A Kentucky native, he served in the War of 1812 and the Creek Indian War, becoming a lieutenant colonel. He moved to Texas in 1839 and taught school at La Grange, later settling at Gay Hill. That same year he embraced Christianity. With W. M. Tryon and J. G. Thomas, he worked to start Baylor University. He was an associate judge of the republic's supreme court and was a district judge during statehood. You'll see a marker for R. E. B. Baylor if you choose to visit the site of **Windmill Hill,** just north of the Antique Rose Emporium that you passed on Highway 50, slightly south of the intersection with 390.

Still at Baylor Park, you'll see a marker for **Horace G. Clark**, who alongside his wife, Martha Davis Clark, was principal and the second president of Baylor Female College. The *Handbook of Texas Online* tells us that he was born in Massachusetts and came to Texas in 1850. Clark was instrumental in building the three-story main hall. He was ordained to the ministry at Independence Baptist Church in 1858. In 1880, Dr. Clark took Holy Orders from Christ Episcopal Church in downtown Houston. Be sure to read the various historic plaques on the property.

When you've finished touring the site turn around and head east on 390. Just east of the intersection with Highway 50, you'll see a prominent two-story white house on your right, 🛑 **Stop 3. Margaret Houston** lived here as a widow from 1863 until her death in 1867.

On the left side of the highway you'll see several markers, including one for **Hood's Texas Brigade**, which is covered in the Civil War chapter. The brigade was raised here in August 1861, as the Texas Aides, by Captain J. B. Robertson. The unit fought in some of the most important battles of the Civil War, including Gaines Mill, Second Manassas, Antietam, Gettysburg, Chickamauga, and the Wilderness.

Continuing east on 390, you can see the **Seward Plantation,** 🛑 **Stop 4**, on your left at 10005 FM 390 East. John Seward came to Texas in 1832 with his father, who was one of Stephen F. Austin's first colonists. The home dates from 1850. It is still owned by Seward family members.

Continue east on Highway 390. In a few miles you'll see a prominent yellow arrow pointing to the right. Rather than doing that, turn left on **William Penn Road**. (Don't worry, it will be paved the whole way, and it's a pretty drive.) If you miss this turn, it's okay; you'll just be adding a few miles. After several miles on William Penn you'll come to an unmarked T intersection, which is Highway 105. Turn left heading northeast on Highway 105. Follow the brown signs into Washington-on-the-Brazos State Park.

If you're wondering about the name William Penn: according to www. texasescapes.com, it comes from a riverboat called *William Penn*, which in turn was named in honor of the Quaker who founded Pennsylvania.

The **museum complex at Washington-on-the-Brazos,** (STOP) **Stop 5**, is excellent. It's worth buying the combination ticket to see all the sites, including the thirty- to forty-five-minute guided tour of Independence Hall, which generally is offered at 11:00 a.m. and 1:00, 2:00, and 3:00 p.m. In total, there are **three sites within the park** in addition to the visitor center: **Independence Hall** and the nearby town site of Washington; the **Star of Texas Museum**; and **Barrington Living History Farm**. All are worth seeing. Be sure to spend time at the visitor center/bookstore during your visit. The book collection and maps are quite good, and there is a nearby exhibit on the background of the revolution.

Independence Hall is a replica of the building where the Texas Declaration of Independence was signed and the Constitution was finalized after seventeen days and nights' work by the fifty-nine delegates. They knew that signing the declaration was akin to signing their own death warrants, should Santa Anna's forward momentum continue. Several days into their deliberations, news of the Alamo's fall created a sense of urgency. The delegates had leased the facility for three months, but they finished the documents in a fraction of that time.

At the visitor center you can see a copy of the Declaration. Janice, a park ranger and guide, has done a significant amount of work researching the signers' lives, and she is happy to share that information with visitors. In **Appendix A** of this book is a **list of the signers**, their municipalities, dates of birth and death, birthplaces, ages at signing, and dates of coming to Texas. Interestingly, Sam Houston was a delegate from Refugio, rather than his Texas residence of Nacogdoches. It turns out he didn't have the necessary votes in Nacogdoches, so he pulled some strings in Refugio, where he was well connected. Harrisburg—now part of the city of Houston—sent three delegates, including the Mexican-born Lorenzo de Zavala, who later became vice president of the Republic of Texas.

Today's traveler to the state park might wonder what happened to the town of Washington-on-the-Brazos, which was becoming a trade center of some renown at the time of the convention. According to information offered during the tour, Washington citizens turned down the railroad, believing that the river would provide enough transportation. They did not want to pay the eleven thousand dollars required by the Houston and Texas Central Railroad. Washington's loss was Navasota's gain. Currently, Navasota's population is about seven thousand, compared to a handful in Washington.

The **Star of Texas Museum** has interesting artifacts and shows exhibits relating to life during revolutionary times. It also shows a twenty-minute film that's worth seeing.

Barrington Plantation is named for its owner and occupant **Anson Jones'** birthplace in Massachusetts. This house, built in 1844 and moved to the current site in 1936, was "the White House of Texas" from 1844 to 1846, during which time Jones was the last president of the Republic of Texas. He retired there after Texas was annexed by the United States. Today, the plantation is part of a living history farm with various types of animals, including hogs, cattle, and poultry, and several gardens that grow heirloom vegetables.

Jones' wife Mary was originally from Alabama. He met her in Houston, where her parents ran a boarding house. They had four children. Two served in the Confederate Army during the Civil War. Sadly, Jones committed suicide in 1858 in Houston at the Capitol Hotel (now the Rice Lofts). He had been subject to depression throughout his life and was distressed that his political career was over.

After touring the plantation, from Washington, take TX 105 East for seven and a half miles until it crosses Highway 6 and becomes TX 90 at Navasota.

As previously mentioned, if you're hungry before you reach Anderson, go north on the Highway 6 feeder at Navasota for a brief time, until you see Martha's Bloomers on your right, set back from the road with a large parking lot in front. The restaurant, **Café M. Bloomers**, is in the rear. The food is very good, and the servings are generous.

If you're running out of time and/or energy here, return to Houston by going south on Highway 6 to Highway 290. You can visit Anderson in conjunction with our Navasota itinerary in chapter 4.

To continue on, go an additional eight miles on Highway 90 to **Anderson, Texas, Stop 6**. On the way, about one and a half miles east of Navasota and across from the Cow Talk Café/Navasota cattle auction house, is an **1859 plantation house**, built with lumber from east Texas sawmills. Now known as the **Foster home**, its original owner was Malcolm Camp, a wealthy cotton planter.

Anderson's history spans the entire period of Anglo settlement in Texas. It is on the road originally used by Spanish explorer **Alonso de Leon** in 1690. In 1821 Andrew Millican began settlement. Heroes of the Texas Revolution lived here, including Tapley Holland and Benjamin Goodrich—the latter of whom signed the Texas Declaration of Independence. Sam Houston, Stephen F. Austin, and General Ulysses S. Grant all visited here. (Grant and Lee both served in the US-Mexican War in the late 1840s.)

This community, originally called Alta Mira or High View, was deemed by some to be the Athens or the Rome of Texas. It housed two universities and one of the earliest newspapers in the state, and there were many well-designed homes. It was a major crossroads for stagecoaches in early Texas. Stage lines from Houston to Old Springfield and from Nacogdoches to Waterloo (later renamed Austin) crossed here. The name of the town changed when K. L. Anderson, the last vice president of the Republic of Texas, died at the Fanthorp Inn. The town's prospects dimmed considerably when railroad lines went through Navasota and bypassed Anderson in the 1850s. (This information was provided by the *Handbook of Texas Online* and the tour guide at the Fanthorp Inn.)

The historic district is on the right side of Highway 90. Upon entering Anderson, bear right on loop 429, and turn right on South Main to visit the **Fanthorp Inn**.

Henry Fanthorp, an immigrant from England, was the most prominent resident in the town's early days. He built the original part of this structure—a one-story "dogtrot"—for his bride, Rachel Kennard, in 1834. Later it was enlarged to become a hotel. Sam Houston, a friend of Fanthorp, stayed many times in the large bedroom downstairs. This building also served as the first mercantile establishment and first post office in the area.

Before returning to Highway 90, go up Main St. toward the Victorian courthouse. On your right, not far from the Fanthorp Inn, is the Greek Revival–style **Anderson Baptist Church**, the roots of which go back to 1855.

The **courthouse** dates from 1891. Be sure to read the various markers on the grounds. One marker notes that Grimes County was named in honor of **Jesse Grimes** (1788–1866), who was a signer of the Texas Declaration of Independence.

During the **Civil War**, this area was a concentration point for troops and ordnance. Anderson sent five cavalry and four infantry companies to the Confederate Army. A munitions factory was located about three miles from here.

From Anderson, turn left (heading west) onto Highway 90 and drive until you reach Highway 6.

✂ If you're returning to Houston, from Highway 90 West, turn left to head south on Highway 6 to reach Highway 290.

There's one more worthwhile stop, though, at the site of **Groce's Retreat/ Retreat Hill Winery**, 🛑 **Stop 7**. Call ahead to see if the winery is open: 936.825.8282. From Anderson, proceed to the intersection of Highway 90 and Highway 6 and turn left, heading south on Highway 6. After about a mile and a half on Highway 6 turn left (to head east) onto TX 105. After almost five miles turn right onto FM 362. In about five miles on your left is Retreat Hill Winery.

Owner Billy S. Cox Jr. can tell you more about the role Groce's Retreat played in the birth of Texas. He also has an excellent map of the Republic of Texas on display in the tasting room. His wine has won several awards, including medals from the Houston Livestock Show and Rodeo and the Finger Lakes competition in New York. Check out his t-shirts, specially designed to commemorate the "come and get it" episode leading to the Texas Revolution.

To return to Houston from Retreat Hill, continue south on FM 362 to reach Highway 290. Return to Houston by heading east on Highway 290.

Itinerary 4: Brazoria County: The Republic's First Capital and the Stephen F. Austin Statue -With optional trip onto Galveston Island

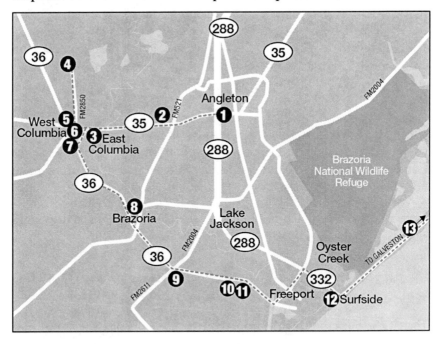

1. Statue of Stephen F. Austin	8. Brazoria
2. Munson Cemetery	9. Ellerslie and Oakland Plantations
3. East Columbia	10. Gulf Prairie Cemetery
4. Varner-Hogg Plantation	11. Durazno Plantation
5. Replica of the first capitol	12. Surfside
6. Rosenwald School	13. Galveston Island
7. Old Columbia Cemetery	